I0811852

Ben's Bug Collection

Understanding Addition

Scott Adams

ROSEN
COMMON CORE MATH
READERS

Rosen Classroom™

New York

Published in 2014 by The Rosen Publishing Group, Inc.
29 East 21st Street, New York, NY 10010

Book Design: Jon D'Rozario

Photo Credits: Cover Jonathan Kirn/The Image Bank/Getty Images; p. 5 Spike Mafford/Photodisc/Getty Images; p. 7 Hemera/ThinkStock.com; p. 9 iStockphoto/ThinkStock.com; p. 11 Eric Isselee/Shutterstock.com; p. 13 Hemera Technologies/ThinkStock.com; p. 15 2happy/Shutterstock.com.

ISBN:978-1-4777-1620-5
6-pack ISBN:978-1-4777-1621-2

Manufactured in the United States of America

CPSIA Compliance Information: Batch #CS13RC: For further information contact Rosen Publishing, New York, New York at 1-800-237-9932.

Word Count: 99

Contents

Ben likes to find bugs in his backyard. He has a big bug collection!

Ben has 5 dragonflies
in his collection.
Then, he finds 3 more.
Now, he has 8 dragonflies.

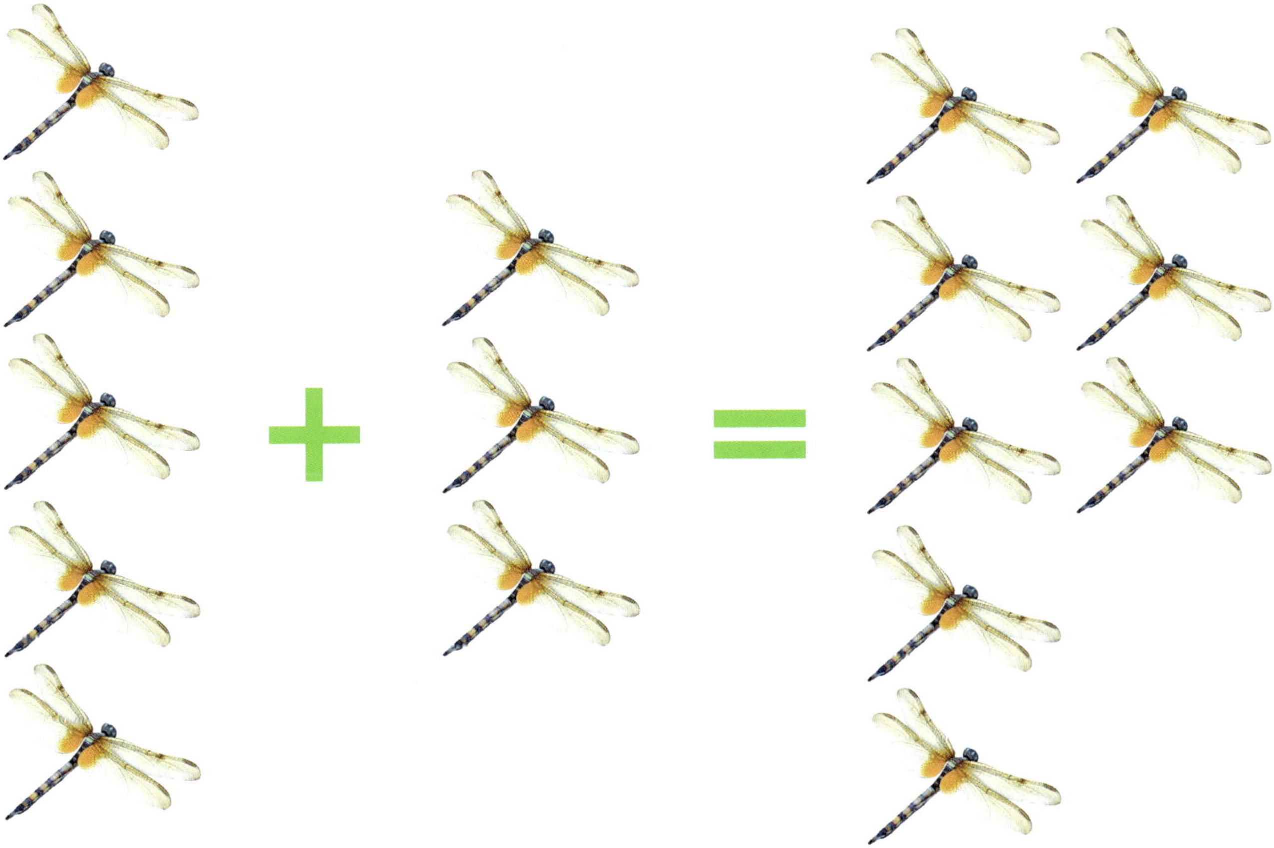

5 + 3 = 8

Ben finds 4 beetles in the grass.
Then, he finds 1 more.
Now, Ben has 5 beetles.

$$4 + 1 = 5$$

There are 7 crickets
in Ben's bug collection.
Then, Ben finds 2 more.
Now, Ben has 9 crickets.

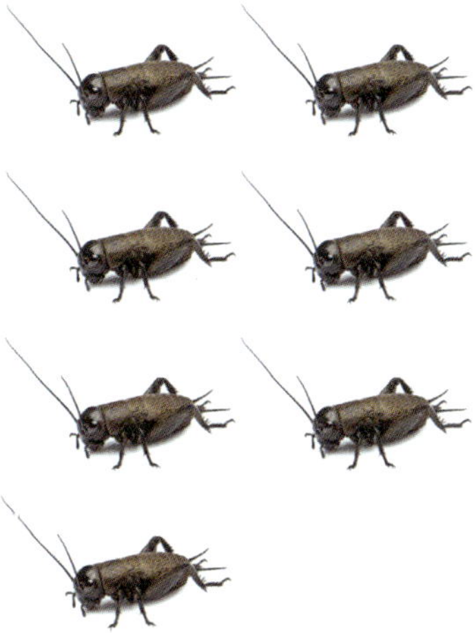 +  = 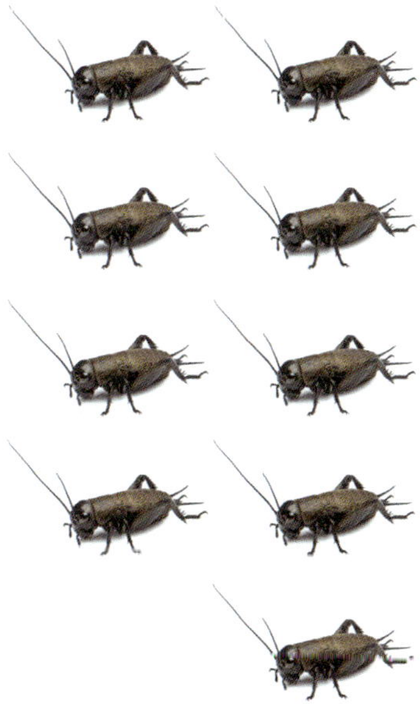

$$7 + 2 = 9$$

Ben has 2 jars to hold spiders.
Then, he gets 3 more jars.
Now, he has 5 jars for spiders.

2 + 3 = 5

Ben collects 5 spiders.
His sister collects 5 more.
That makes 10 spiders!

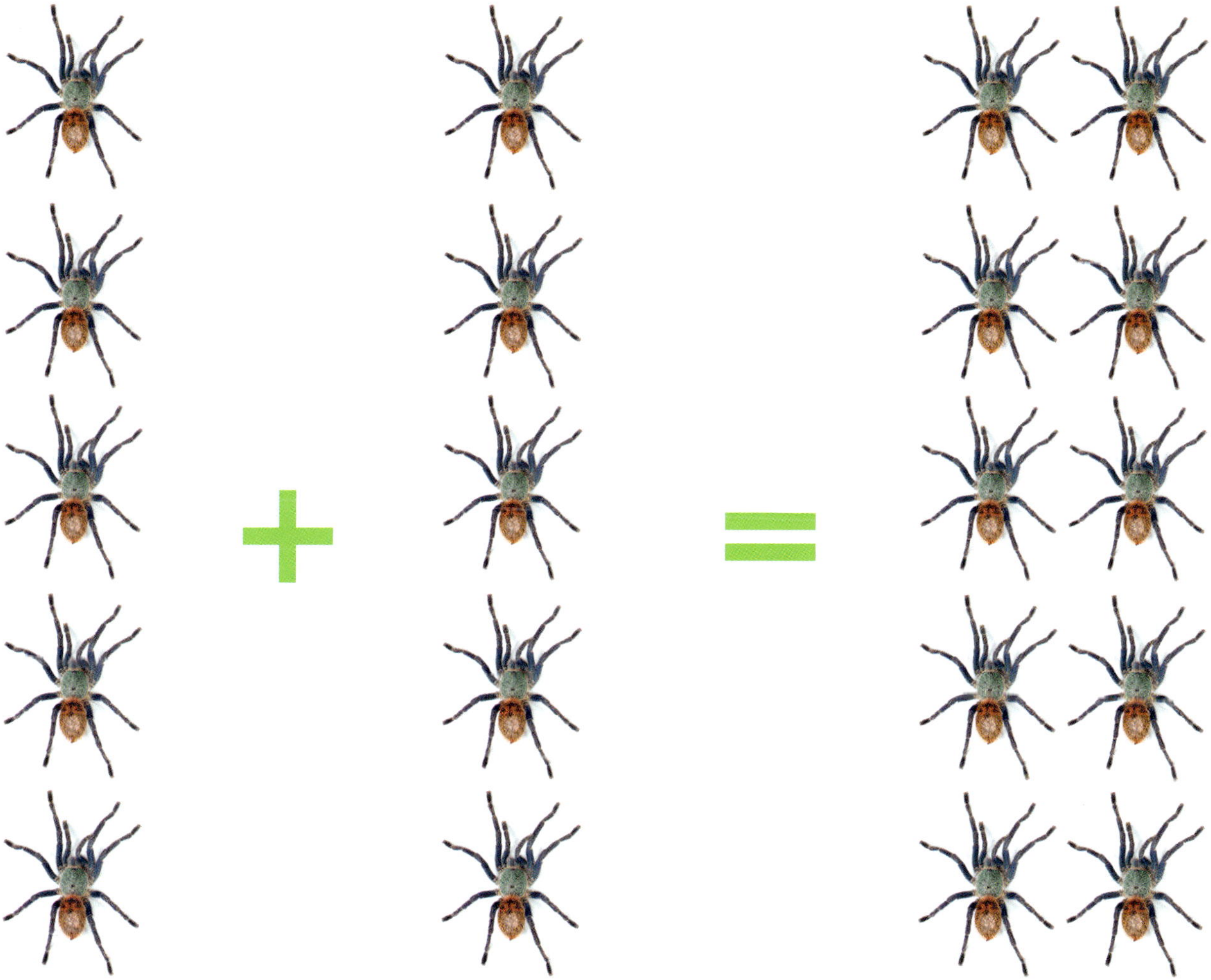

$5 + 5 = 10$

Words to Know

beetle

cricket

dragonfly

spider

Index